£50

Reincarnation:

Rein-carnation:
Fact or Fallacy?

Geoffrey Hodson

This publication made possible with
the assistance of the Kern Foundation
The Theosophical Publishing House
Wheaton, Ill. U.S.A.
Madras, India / London, England

© Copyright 1967, The Theosophical Publishing House

All rights reserved.

First Quest Book edition (revised), 1967, published by the Theosophical Publishing House, a department of the Theosophical Society in America.

Third Quest printing 1979.

ISBN: 0-8356-0046-7.
Library of Congress Catalog Card Number 67-4405

Printed in the United States of America

As when with downcast eyes we muse and brood,
And ebb into a former life, or seem
To lapse far back in some confused dream
To states of mystical similitude,
If one but speaks or hems or stirs his chair
Ever the wonder waxeth more and more,
So that we say, "All this hath been before,
All this hath been, I know not when or where;"
So, friend, when first I look'd upon your face,
Our thought gave answer each to each, so true —
Opposed mirrors each reflecting each —
That, tho' I knew not in what time or place,
Methought that I had often met with you,
And either lived in either's heart and speech.

ALFRED, LORD TENNYSON.

ACKNOWLEDGMENTS

WE wish to express our gratitude to the following for their kindness in giving permission for the use of copyright materials:

George G. Harrap and Co. Ltd., London, and Harcourt, Brace and Company, Inc., New York, for the passage from *Adventures in Arabia* by W. B. Seabrook; The Editor, *Answers* of London, for "This Boy Had Lived Before"; The Editor, *Reader's Digest* and Donald Culross Peattie for "Mozart, Music's Wonder Child"; The Editor, *American Magazine,* for quotation from "The Most Extraordinary Coincidence I know of" from a letter by R. A.; Macmillan and Co. Ltd., London, for the excerpt from *The Soul of a People* by H. Fielding Hall; The Editor, *The Aryan Path* for quotations from "Reasonableness and Practicality of Reincarnation" by John Middleton Murry, and "On Reincarnation" by Algernon Blackwood; and Hutchison Publishing Group Ltd., London, for excerpt from *Pythagoras and the Delphic Mysteries* by Edouard Schuré.

PUBLISHERS

ACKNOWLEDGMENTS

TABLE OF CONTENTS

TABLE OF CONTENTS

CHAPTER I

FOUR MAJOR PROBLEMS

THIS book is written in exposition of the doctrine, accepted as true by countless millions of people from the remotest time, that man evolves spiritually to perfection by means of successive lives on earth. In various forms this belief has proved and is still proving to be a consolation and an inspiration to vast multitudes of people. The doctrine of rebirth is, therefore, well worthy of investigation.

Direct spiritual perception apart, what test of verity can be applied? How may the truth or untruth of reincarnation be established? Reason and intuition may be employed, but there is also another test — that of application to certain basic problems of life, and this I endeavor to indicate.

JUSTICE

The first of these problems is that of justice in human affairs, of the combined existence of apparently undeserved human suffering — especially of little children — and of divine justice. Dryden posed this question by affirming that "Virtue in distress and vice in triumph make atheists of mankind." Undoubtedly the occurrence and the continuance of human suffering for which no commensurate transgression is known, do appear to deny the existence of a principle of equity.

Concerning this first problem, Christian peoples are informed and are ready to believe that the God who reigns above and within them is a just God and further that his justice, while absolute, is yet ever tempered with mercy. God's law is said to be administered with divine tenderness for all that he has made. "God . . . will not suffer you to be tempted above that ye are able; but will with the temptation also make a way to escape, that ye may be able to bear it."[1] God notes each sparrow's fall.[2] The heart answers to this belief. Instinctively the soul of man is ready to believe in, and with reverent love to worship, a God of divine justice and compassion, an all-loving Father in heaven.

Nevertheless, no one at all observant of common human experience, especially that of suffering, can deny at least the appearance of the most cruel injustice in human affairs. No thoughtful individual can long be blind, for example, to the inequalities of health and opportunity under which children are innocently and helplessly born. In this, as in so much else, one must confess to the appearance of inequity. Some children are born with healthy bodies and in happy homes, where they are loved, cared for and provided with opportunities for their happiness and progress in life, while millions of other children are born into conditions of the greatest difficulty. The bodies of some of them are malformed, tainted with disease. Others are born blind, deaf and dumb, apparently condemned from birth to lives of the greatest limitation, if not misery. Still other children are born into homes of vice, poverty, dirt and disease; they are unloved from birth, hungry, neglected, and beaten as they grow up. They start life

1I Cor. X, 13.
2Matt. X, 29.

with the severest handicaps and some of them develop into hardened criminals.

Observing this one phenomenon alone, of the inequalities of birth, the mind can hardly avoid the question: "If there be a God of justice, of love and of compassion, why then does he permit the agelong and unchanging continuance of such cruel injustice? Why do millions of his children come down from heaven to earth into conditions under which health, happiness and fulfillment are virtually impossible to them?" Such, in part, is the first great problem — that of apparent injustice in the world.

DESTINY

The second question concerns the meaning, the purpose and the ultimate goal of human existence, if goal there be. We may brand as pessimists those who recognize the uncertainty and the apparent hopelessness and purposelessness of human life; but such branding does not answer the question to which they draw attention; for this second problem arises from the fact that for a large proportion of the human race, life is lived under the perpetual shadow of fear, resulting from the danger of financial insecurity, disease, depression and war. The so-called pessimist has grounds for the questions: "What hope is there in a life which may at any moment either be rendered insupportable or be swept away? What future can there be for a humanity which is continually decimated by war, pestilence, flood, famine and disease? What light is there to be found in a world which is so overshadowed by these dark clouds? What value or purpose can there be in such a life?"

PRODIGIES AND TRUE MEMORIES

The third problem is that of the existence of child prodigies, young boys and girls who display a virtuosity explainable neither by heredity nor preceding experience. The fourth enigma is presented by the considerable number of people who claim to remember their past lives, their recollections in some cases being supported by their relation of historical facts of which they could not otherwise have become aware.

Such are four of the great questions confronting mankind to which as a means of testing their verity, I propose to apply the doctrines of reincarnation and compensatory law.

CHAPTER II

THEIR SOLUTION

IN offering a solution of the four problems stated in the preceding chapter, I shall draw on that accumulated and inherited wisdom of the ages, known even in olden days as the Ancient Wisdom, named by Greek philosophers at Alexandria *Theosophia* which means Divine Wisdom, and known in modern days as Theosophy. For these are no new problems. The human mind has noted and sought to solve them from the dawn of man's power to observe, to reason and to inquire.

In advance, I may say that the Ancient Wisdom teaches that divine justice *does* rule the world and that there *is* a meaning and a purpose behind human life. Despite the appearance of injustice, perfect justice is, in fact, insured to every human being by the operation of a compensatory law, the law of cause and effect known in the East as *karma*.

PERFECTED MANHOOD

The purpose of life is stated to be the evolution of the human soul, the Spiritual Self, to the stature of the perfect man, a state of complete fulfillment and highest development, defined by St. Paul in Ephesians IV. 13 in these words: "Till we all come in the unity of the faith, and of the knowledge of the Son of God, unto a perfect man, unto the measure of the stature of the fullness of Christ." Such, according to Theosophy also, is the goal of human life — to come "unto the measure of the stature of the fullness of Christ." That is why we are here; that is the great deliverance to which we are all journeying. That is why we endure our manifold afflictions and experience our upliftments and our joys. All these are the means whereby the divine powers, potentially present within the soul of man from the beginning, germinate and develop from the seed-like to the fully unfolded state.

The Ancient Wisdom also affirms that this attainment of perfection is utterly certain for the Spiritual Soul of every human being. One day all will obey the command given in the Bible, "Be ye therefore perfect, even as your Father which is in heaven is perfect."[1]

THE TIME PROBLEM

Nevertheless, the problems of the necessary time and the opportunities inevitably present themselves to the thoughtful mind; for no single life, even if of the allotted span, can possibly provide a sufficient number and variety of experiences, challenges and opportunities necessary for the attainment of the stature of the perfect man. The fulfillment of human life — becoming perfect physically and intellectually as well as spiritually — is indeed impossible in one brief human life alone. If but one life there be, then, the task of reaching Christhood is hopeless of fulfillment. Man is foredoomed to failure from the beginning, and this for want of adequate time and opportunity in which to develop to the point of genius every human faculty, to master every weakness, and ultimately to make manifest every God-like power.

[1]Matt. V, 48 (A.V.).

REINCARNATION THE ANSWER

If, however, reincarnation be true, if we do return to earth time and time again, growing a little on each occasion, then the possibility exists of full unfoldment. If at the close of each life we have advanced a few steps — in some very successful lives, perchance many steps — toward the great goal, then at the end of a number of such lives perfection could be achieved. If these are the conditions under which human life is planned and lived, an almost infinite vista opens out before each one of us. We face a future which is full of light and of the promise of spiritual victory. It is not difficult to understand that such a belief in spiritual evolution through successive lives on earth would inspire hope and give confidence and courage to those for whom it is acceptable.

YOUTHFUL GENIUS

Child prodigies who early display remarkable natural faculties enabling them to excel — in mathematics, literature or a branch of the arts, for example — are reincarnations of people who, having achieved mastery in former lives, have brought over their acquired faculties as so-called natural "gifts".

ACCURATE MEMORY

The accurate narration of historical events by those claiming to have participated in them, and who could not have become aware of them by any natural means, is explained as being due to the transference from one body to its successor of the memory of those events. When their stories are put to the test and found to be true, as in the cases referred to in Chapter VI, these people are actually remembering their former lives.

Such, briefly stated, are the solutions of the four problems made possible by the adoption of the doctrines of reincarnation and karma. A fuller exposition of each solution will be given later in this work.

CHAPTER III

PREVALENT OBJECTIONS

ARE the theories of reincarnation and karma really true? Are these age-old doctrines founded upon fact? Such questions must be approached with a completely open mind, for prejudice is one of the greatest barriers to the attainment of knowledge. Is it not a curious fact that while from time immemorial Oriental peoples have accepted reincarnation in one form or another as a basic and unchallengeable fact of life, we of the West hesitate to assent? In order to facilitate unprejudiced examination of the doctrine of rebirth, I now consider some prevalent objections and offer answers to each of them.

REBIRTH NOT DESIRED

One of the commonest objections arises from a shrinking from life in the flesh and from the suffering which is the lot of man at this stage of human evolution. "I don't want to come back here again," so many people say, "once is enough for me!" One cannot but sympathize with those whose experience of life has been so unfortunate as to bring them to such a conclusion. Nevertheless, according to the doctrine of reincarnation the objection is invalid, is misconceived. For by rebirth is not implied the return to earth to our present selves. This personal self with its bodily and mental characteristics, its name, race, creed, sex and outlook — this person does not return. According to Theosophy, at death the temporary mortal body is finally laid aside to reappear no more, the same later becoming true for the bodies of emotion and of mind.[1] That which down here we generally regard as ourselves is, in reality, not our true selves at all. That true Self of man is an eternal, immortal, spiritual being, quite distinct from, even while occupying, the physical body; being immortal and eternal, it does not, cannot die. The body, on the other hand, being but mortal, naturally passes away. Since it had a beginning, it must have an end. The Spiritual Self is permanent, everlasting; never having had a beginning, it can never have an end. This all-important truth is beautifully expressed in Sir Edwin Arnold's poetic translation of the great Hindu Scripture, *The Bhagavad Gita:*

Never the spirit was born; the spirit shall cease to be
     never;
Never was time it was not; End and Beginning are dreams!
Birthless and deathless and changeless remaineth the spirit
     for ever;
Death hath not touched it at all, dead though the house
     of it seems!"

The Song Celestial

According to the doctrine of reincarnation, it is the Divine Self, the immortal pilgrim God within the body, which reincarnates, and not the mortal, bodily man with his transient feelings and thoughts. When, therefore, we think and say in

[1]Vide *Death and After,* A Besant; *Through the Gateway of Death,* Geoffrey Hodson.

objection to rebirth, "I do not want to return," we need have no fear. We, as we normally know ourselves, do not return. It is the divine essence, the Spiritual Self, with its acquired, individual attributes, which reincarnates. This one common objection thus disposed of, one difficulty is, I hope, cleared away.

TRANSMIGRATION

A further objection is based upon the possibility that reincarnation might imply transmigration of souls from human into animal forms. This is an entirely erroneous view of the doctrine and consequently, as an objection, is invalid. When once the life in any form has attained to a certain level of unfoldment, although there may be delay or digression, there is no real retrogression.

COMPULSION

The idea that the process of descent into incarnation could be forced upon us by an external power against our will, is also unacceptable to some minds. To this objection the answer is made that the impulse to descend into a new baby body arises within the Spiritual Self, the reincarnating principle. The expansive pressure of the divine Will, which is the power behind the whole process of evolution throughout the universe, is felt by the human Monad-Ego, the Spiritual Self, as an interior resolve and not as an external, resistless command. As there is but one divine Will, one divine Life and one divine Intelligence — a Trinity in unity — throughout and within all nature and all men, the divine triplicity which constitutes the Dweller in the innermost in man must be part of the one great divinity in all, and not separate in any way therefrom.

In consequence of this basic and indissoluble unity, the impetus to self-expression in material forms for purposes of unfoldment, the thrust of Spirit, is in no sense received externally by the Spiritual Self of man. Interior impulsion and not external compulsion, initiates the process of incarnation in successive forms. There is but one spiritual Will in the cosmos and the Will-Self of the Monad of man is an embodiment thereof. Full recognition of this fact is the highest vision, and its ratification in action is the secret of well-being. Thus it is seen that the Spiritual Self of man voluntarily accepts the opportunity of achieving further evolutionary progress provided by the experiences of earthly life. Self-impelled, the Monad-Ego of man sets forth upon its pilgrimage to perfection. Self-impelled, also, it descends into each new physical form.

SEPARATION OF LOVED ONES

The mind may also shrink from accepting the doctrine of reincarnation on the grounds that rebirth will so separate loved ones as to preclude all possibility of future reunion. This objection, in its turn, is invalid. Neither birth nor death nor rebirth can ever completely or finally separate those between whom a deep spiritual, intellectual or physical bond has been formed. In their spiritual selves, wherein the closest affinity has been established, they are for ever at one, whether physically embodied or disembodied; for in the state of consciousness in which the Spiritual Self of man abides separation is impossible, parting unknown.

Furthermore, the very fact of the existence of so close a bond will cause them repeatedly to descend into incarnation at about the same time, and under conditions in which they are likely to meet, being drawn together by their affinity and the law of cause and effect. On meeting, although the new brain, the seat of memory, may not remember the incidents of past intimate associations, the heart speaks, a mutual attraction is felt and love is renewed, sometimes, indeed, at first sight. Again a life relationship differing in various incarnations is established. This may be parental, filial or — whether within or without the family — fraternal. In each new association love deepens, grows more unselfish, more noble, until at last the state is reached of love perfected, which is life perfected. Even after the human kingdom is left behind and the super-human kingdom entered, there is evidence that the close association continues in that co-operation with the one Will which is characteristic of the life of the Adept.

CHAPTER IV

REINCARNATION AND CHRISTIANITY

MEMBERS of the Christian faith sometimes object to the doctrine of reincarnation on the grounds that to accept it would be a violation of Christian doctrine. While it is true that a Council of Constantinople in the sixth century A. D. pronounced belief in the pre-existence of the soul to be heretical, an examination of the Scriptures strongly suggests that the doctrine of rebirth was generally accepted in those days and that Our Lord himself believed it. Whether this be the case or not, the student of the Christian doctrine may well ask whether a decision made by a group of men in the sixth century should be regarded as binding today.

This objection to reincarnation by Christians, on grounds of doctrinal fidelity, is sufficiently important to merit a somewhat detailed examination. From this it is found that reincarnation has neither been proclaimed nor condemned by any general council of the Church or by any creed accepted by a general council. The Council of Constantinople held in 543 A.D., which proclaimed heretical Origen's teaching of the pre-existence of the soul and affirmed the doctrine of special creation, was not a general council, and so not universally authoritative. It was a local and not an ecumenical council or synod. Furthermore, it did not condemn reincarnation but only pre-existence, which has nothing to do with rebirth. Origen taught that all souls were created at the beginning of creation as angelic spirits. In this condition they sinned and for their apostasy were transferred into material bodies. It was this view of pre-existence which was proclaimed heretical. In any case, heresy thus condemned so long ago need not be regarded today as of major importance. Truth matters a great deal more and a condemned heresy may turn out to be a truth, as happened, for example, when a local church of Rome condemned Galileo's heliocentric doctrine and forced him to recant. Galileo was right and the church in question was wrong. It is therefore quite legitimate for both clergy and laity of the Christian faith to preach and believe in both pre-existence and reincarnation.

ELIJAH AND JOHN THE BAPTIST

The testimony of the Bible itself, although admittedly inconclusive, does suggest a general belief in the doctrine of rebirth at the time of Our Lord. In the Old Testament the prophets foretell the reappearance of one of themselves. Isaiah speaks thus of a forerunner and a Messiah:

> "The voice of him that crieth in the wilderness, Prepare ye the way of the Lord, make straight in the desert a highway for our God." (Isaiah XL.3.)

The Prophet Malachi wrote:

> "Behold, I will send you Elijah, the prophet, before the coming of the great and dreadful day of the Lord." (Malachi IV.5.)

This prophecy is fulfilled in the New Testament. In his first chapter, St. Luke tells of the conception of John the Baptist as promised by the angel to the future father, Zacharias.

Elizabeth, his wife, he was told, would conceive and bear a son. In verse 17 Gabriel proclaims:

> "And he shall go before him in the spirit and power of Elias to turn the hearts of the fathers to the children, and the disobedient to the wisdom of the just; to make ready a people prepared for the Lord." (Luke 1,17.)

Although stricken in years, Elizabeth conceived and according to ancient prophecy John was born, as a forerunner of the Lord, sent in the spirit and power of Elijah. In the sixth month, the same angel, Gabriel, appeared to Mary in Nazareth and foretold the birth of Jesus, who later was born in Bethlehem. In the midst of His ministry, as St. Matthew records, Our Lord, speaking of John the Baptist, said:

> "And as they departed, Jesus began to say unto the multitudes concerning John, What went ye out into the wilderness to see? A reed shaken with the wind?
>
> But what went ye out for to see? A man clothed in soft raiment? Behold, they that wear soft clothing are in king's houses.
>
> But what went ye out for to see? A prophet? Yea, I say unto you, and more than a prophet. For this is he, of whom it is written, Behold, I send my messenger before thy face, which shall prepare thy way before thee.
>
> Verily I say unto you. Among them that are born of women there hath not risen a greater than John the Baptist: notwithstanding he that is least in the kingdom of heaven is greater than he.
>
> And from the days of John the Baptist until now the

kingdom of heaven suffereth violence, and the violent take it by force.

For all the prophets and the law prophesied until John.

And if ye will receive it, this is Elias, which was for to come.

He that hath ears to hear, let him hear."

(Matt. XI, 7-15.)

Later in his Gospel, St. Matthew says:

"When Jesus came into the coasts of Caesarea Philippi, he asked his disciples, saying, Whom do men say that I the Son of man am? And they said, Some say that thou art John the Baptist; some, Elias; and others, Jeremias, or one of the prophets."

(Matt. XVI, 13-14.)

This reply reveals the popular view founded upon both prophecy and a general belief in the possibility of rebirth.

References are to be found in the works of the Jewish historian, Josephus, showing that belief in reincarnation must have been common among Palestinian Jews of that period. His remarks to Jewish soldiers who preferred suicide to capture by the Romans provide an interesting example:

"Do ye not remember that all pure spirits who are in conformity with the divine dispensation lived on in the lowliest of heavenly places, and in course of time they are again sent down to inhabit sinless bodies; but the souls of those who have committed self-destruction are doomed to a region of darkness in the underworld?"

(De Bello Judaico)

This is also made obvious in the instance of the man born blind:

> "And as Jesus passed by, he saw a man which was blind from his birth.
>
> And his disciples asked him, saying Master, who did sin, this man, or his parents, that he was born blind?
>
> Jesus answered, Neither hath this man sinned, nor his parents: but that the works of God should be made manifest in him."

(John IX, 1-3.)

The question as to whether the man himself had sinned and in consequence had been born sightless shows the clear thought that justice demanded that the transgression should have occurred in a physical body. As this could only have happened in a former life on earth, belief in reincarnation is implicit in the question. Our Lord's answer, which appears to deny rebirth, is susceptible of more than one interpretation. It is technically correct to say that the new personality, with its name, nationality and characteristics, was not responsible for the actions of which his blindness was the result. The actor was distinctly another man with another name and personality, even though the Spiritual Soul within both bodies was the same. The identity or sameness is not of bodily person but of the God within which is undergoing a pilgrimage toward perfection in order that, as Our Lord further said, "the works of God should be made manifest in him."

Although the question obviously implies belief in, or at least knowledge of, reincarnation on the part of the questioners, the answer given by Christ by no means implies denial of the truth of that doctrine. Rather does it seem to concede the point, for the disciples were not rebuked nor was the implication denied. The interrogators were informed that in this particular case prenatal sin was not the cause of the blindness. It may have come upon the man from other causes. The inner Self may possibly have accepted physical blindness to assist him in the inward search for truth, even to drive him thereto in the new body, blindness being regarded by it rather as a help than a punishment. Or it may be that blindness was accepted somewhat vicariously for the fulfillment of some spiritual purpose. Greatness of soul does appear to be indicated in later verses of the same chapter in which, despite the rule that any man who confessed that Jesus was the Christ should be put out of the synagogue (John IX, 22.), the man who was healed stoutly affirmed the fact. Furthermore, when he was expelled and Jesus sought him out and conversed with him, his spiritual insight was sufficient to enable him to say "Lord, I believe," and thereafter to worship the Christ.

When considering this question, it should also be remembered that the Bible is written in the language of symbols, a special category of literature designed both to conceal and to reveal spiritual truths. Blindness is a symbol for temporary unawareness of spiritual light. The Christ partly represents spiritual intuitiveness. When one who is spiritually blind becomes intuitively awakened and active or, symbolically, enters the presence of the Christ and is healed by him, the scales are said to have fallen from his eyes. This I believe to be the true symbolical interpretation; for I look upon the story as one of the many beautiful miniature mystery dramas to be found in the Bible, portraying in allegory and symbol the soul's awakening from darkness to light. Nevertheless, symbolism apart, the answer given by the Lord was, as stated above, doctrinally and technically correct.

The disciples later asked the Master why it had been written that Elijah should appear first, and received a remarkable reply. St. Matthew records the incident thus:

> "And his disciples asked him, saying, Why then say the scribes that Elias must first come?
>
> And Jesus answered and said unto them, Elias truly shall first come, and restore all things.
>
> But I say unto you, that Elias is come already, and they knew him not, but have done unto him whatsoever they listed. Likewise shall also the Son of man suffer of them.
>
> Then the disciples understood that he spake unto them of John the Baptist."
>
> (Matt. XVII, 10-13.)

St. Mark repeats this:
> "But I say unto you, that Elias is indeed come, and they have done unto him whatsoever they listed, as it is written of him."
>
> (Mark IX, 13.)

This is unequivocal and inescapable. It is the reincarnation of Elijah, foretold by a prophet, believed in by the Jewish people and affirmed by Jesus, the Christ. Elijah, who had been translated to heaven many centuries before, had returned to earth as John the Baptist, assuming a new physical body which displayed certain characteristics of his previous incarnation, particularly ruggedness of appearance and "a girdle of leather about his loins". (2 Kings I, 8 and Matt. III, 4.)

John the Baptist himself denied that he was Elijah. (John I, 21-25.) It is, however, very unusual for any person to remember former lives before the attainment of a certain degree of spiritual and occult development. Our Lord spoke with superior knowledge and also said that although John was a great prophet, "he that is least in the kingdom of heaven is greater than he." (Matt. XI, 11.) This suggests that John was not comparable in spiritual stature to an initiate,[1] even of the first degree. This statement by Our Lord is somewhat supported in the Epistle of James V, 17: "Elias was a man subject to like passions as we are." Under these conditions, it is not at all surprising that John should have no recollection of his past lives, and in any case his denial would not have the same weight as the affirmation made by Our Lord himself.

THE SINS OF THE FATHERS

In the second commandment, God is made to say that he visits "the iniquity of the fathers upon the children unto the third and fourth generation". (Exodus XX, 5.) Those who hold the doctrine of reincarnation sometimes speak of the personalities of preceding lives as the parents of those which follow, somewhat in the same sense in which a proverb states "The boy is father to the man," meaning that the boy is the man in embryo. Similarly, each life is the product of its predecessors, particularly as regards inborn capacities, quali-

[1] Vide *Initiation, the Perfecting of Man*, A. Besant.

ties of character and special faculties. Taken thus, the statement is strictly true.

If, on the other hand, there be but one life and the children who are made to suffer for their fathers' iniquities are entirely different spiritual souls, then the enactment of a grotesque and barbarous injustice is attributed to the All-Father; atheism or agnosticism would be preferable, for as Bacon said: "It is better to have no opinion at all of God than such an opinion as is unworthy of him, for the one is unbelief, the other is contumely." If, however, the Biblical statement is regarded in the reincarnationist sense that man reaps in his present body the fruits and results of actions committed in bodies worn in previous lives, then the words attributed to God become a statement of ideal justice. A great Theosophist and seeress has written:

> "The Ancient Wisdom tells us that somewhere in the memory of Nature every act of each one of her children is self-engraved, and that from this self-written record under the guidance of Angelic Ministers, the changing destiny of men and nations flows. Thus is it claimed that our present attainments of talent and capacity are what we have won in the past; that our present thoughts and activities will determine our future, and that in the sum of things nowhere is there any injustice, and nowhere caprice or favoritism."
>
> *Annie Besant*

THE ATTAINMENT OF PERFECTION

Reference has already been made to the command given

by Christ to his followers: "Be ye therefore perfect, even as your Father which is in heaven is perfect." (Matt. V, 48.) If man is granted but one life in which to accomplish this perfection, such attainment would be an impossibility for almost every human being; and Our Lord would have presented to mankind an ideal which is impossible of fulfillment. Since his wisdom was perfect, it is extremely unlikely that he would have taken this course. If, however, each man is granted almost unlimited time and every needed opportunity throughout successive lives in which to reach the goal which is set for him, then Our Lord's words are less an injunction than a description of the destiny of every man. Indeed, in the original Greek and in the Revised Version, the behest becomes a simple statement of fact: "Ye therefore shall be perfect, as your heavenly Father is perfect."

CHAPTER V

THE VARIABILITY
OF CHRISTIAN DOGMAS

A STUDY of Christian origins and of the history of the Church since the first century, reveals that many changes have occurred in the number and nature of beliefs held as essentials of the Christian religion by certain Christian bodies. The geocentric system is an example of a firmly held article of faith, disbelief in which, as in the case of Galileo, was regarded as heretical. Other beliefs have either undergone changes or have disappeared, evolving man having outgrown them. It is clear, therefore, that they never were beliefs necessary for salvation, and that some of them simply were not true. In consequence, it cannot with reason and justice be claimed that other doctrines may only be interpreted in the literal and present-day sense by those who profess to be Christians.

This leaves the whole question of what does and what does not constitute Christian orthodoxy in a very fluid state. Indeed, many people at the present time are finding difficulty in accepting as literally and finally true such dogma as the infallibility of the Old and New Testaments; that all mankind descended from one pair of original parents; that their procreative act constituted a fall or grave sin which has been handed down to the whole human race ever since as "original sin" by which every single member of the race has been stained; that after some thousands of years the Supreme Deity sent his only Son down to earth in order that the harm done by the iniquity of the first pair might be undone and mankind thus be ransomed by a kind of bribe to Satan and set free from his otherwise rightful hold upon it; that to prevent this original sin from reaching the Lord Christ, who was both man and God, he was born of a virgin who had miraculously conceived; that the consummation of the redemptive process consisted of his crucifixion by the Jews, after which his body was raised from the tomb and later ascended into heaven; that in consequence of this sacrifice all those — and presumably only those — who were able to affirm belief in this group of ideas before they died would after death be washed white and clean "in the blood of the Lamb" and the normal operation of the law of cause and effect would be abrogated in their case, and that all who did not so affirm were, in all probability, condemned to eternal damnation, one concomitant of which is to be perpetually burned in the fires of hell,[1] and another to become outcasts from God's love of the human race.

Admittedly this theological structure can grant no place to the twin doctrines enunciated by both Our Lord and St. Paul,[2] of the spiritual evolution of the soul of every man to the "measure of the stature of the fullness of Christ" by means of successive lives and of the operation of the law of cause and effect. If belief in the fall and redemption of man according to these doctrines be the unchanging and unfailing hallmark of the true Christian, then indeed neither reincarnation nor karma can be regarded as acceptable by churches established

[1] The concept of the existence in the superphysical worlds of physical fire which can burn, and so punish, is indeed an anomaly.

[2] For references, see Chapter X.

in such belief. Yet, certain Christian denominations and individual Christians, believing that they may lawfully profess and call themselves Christians, do not adhere to the literal reading of this set of doctrines. Some of them find an allegorical and mystical meaning which permits a conviction that no spiritual soul, whatever his belief, can ever be lost or ever excluded from the love of God and "that all his sons shall one day reach his feet, however far they stray". *An act of Faith* of the Liberal Catholic Church, from which the phrase is taken, reads as follows:

"We believe that God is Love, and Power, and Truth, and Light; that perfect justice rules the world: that all His sons shall one day reach His Feet, however far they stray. We hold the Fatherhood of God, the Brotherhood of man; we know that we do serve Him best when best we serve our brother man. So shall His blessing rest on us, and peace for evermore."

The majority of the members of this communion accept the doctrines of the eternity and immortality of the soul of man; the perfectibility of man; the atonement of Christ as a perpetual interior experience in which the soul continually receives his outpoured, perfected light, life and grace, thereby being cleansed and saved from far worse error and consequent suffering than would otherwise be the case, and in the operation of an immutable and inviolable law of cause and effect under which absolute justice is assured to every human being, both in the physical and superphysical worlds.

THE TRUE NATURE OF RELIGION

Since the question of whether or not reincarnation is really contrary to Christian teaching may well be the deciding factor in its acceptance or rejection, the true nature of religion must now be briefly considered. What is religion? What is the nature of faith? Religion, surely, is not only a question of adherence to doctrines, dogmas, creeds and observances, it is also an experience in consciousness. At its highest that experience is an ecstasy of union with God, a merging of the individual light in the radiance of the Supreme. In action, religion is service motived by love. The essential of any faith is to live the life, and the Christian life can be simply described by such sentences as: "Christ is our foundation"; "Do unto others as you would they should do unto you"; "Seek those things which are above, where Christ sitteth at the right hand of God"; "Ye shall be perfect as your Father in heaven is perfect"; "The true light (Divine Light) which lighteth every man that cometh into the world." To these may be added the assurance that one day the light which lighteth every man will be consciously merged with the infinite light of God.

A deep religious philosophy of life which can be justified at the bar of the intellect is an ever-present, human need. In its highest essence, in its original purity, Christianity meets that need by its revelation of the living light which the great Founder brought to men nearly 2,000 years ago. Despite the changes and accretions of the intervening centuries, that light still shines. Men and women of every walk of life, humble and exalted, have borne witness to its shining and to their direct awareness of the Divine Presence and Power. Spiritual light is not dependent for its illuminating power upon knowledge and acceptance of the dogmas of any particular creed.

Perception of spiritual truth calls for no blind obedience, no enslavement of the reasoning mind. Rather does spiritual truth demand for its reception a free, unfettered, active but reverent mind and an awakened intuition. For it is there, in the highest parts of man's nature, that the existence of the Divine in all creation, and therefore within every man, may be realized and known. To the heart that is responsive to the suffering of the world, to the active mind aspiring to wisdom, to the intuition that is awake, the Divine Presence is ever revealed, the Divine Voice forever speaks. Realization of that unfailing Presence, response to that inner voice — these alone are the essentials of a faith which can never fail. Original Christianity as portrayed in the New Testament is a revelation of that faith. By this standard and the quoted evidence of the Bible itself, no violence is done to the Christian orthodoxy by acceptance of the doctrine of rebirth.

CHAPTER VI

THE MEMORY OF FORMER LIVES

A FURTHER objection to reincarnation is based upon the apparent absence of all memory of past lives. A little reflection, however, will show that recollection of the process of education is in no sense essential to possession of the acquired knowledge and faculty. We do not need to remember the processes of learning to walk, talk, read and write, in order to be able to do these things. Similarly, the absence of memory of incidents and experiences in past lives does not prevent the use of the resultant powers in later incarnations. Actually the reincarnating ego does retain both the full memory of all incidents of past life cycles and all the capacities attained. Furthermore, just as remembrance of childish struggles when learning to walk, talk, read and write is rarely retained in adult life, so recollection of the multifarious educative experiences of numerous preceding lives is not permitted to descend into the new mind-brain. In consequence, the weight of the drama of previous existences is withheld and the mind left free to investigate and assimilate new ideas. This withholding of memory may have been implied by classical reference to the river Lethe in the lower world, the waters of which gave forgetfulness of the past. The fruits of past lives are expressed, however, in each new personality as instinct and inherent "gifts," as sympathies and antipathies and as the voice of conscience.

Furthermore, as will now be shown, many proven cases of accurate memory of former lives have been recorded. The solution of the fourth problem presented by those who claim to remember past lives, now emerges: it is that in certain cases such memories are true, and thereby constitute strong additional evidence in support of the doctrine of rebirth.

REGRESSION OF MEMORY

While the only final proof of the truth of the doctrine of reincarnation consists of direct knowledge of one's own past lives, convincing evidence is provided by Colonel de Rochas in his book, *Les Vies Successives*. Therein he describes experiments with various sensitives put into a trance state by hypnotism. By the process known as regression of memory, the operators succeeded in taking their subjects back to their former incarnations, thus obtaining details, often of a historical character, which, when checked later, were found to be entirely correct.

In one typical instance, the sensitive chosen for an experiment was a young servant girl with little or no education and but a rudimentary knowledge of history who, when taken back to her preceding life, described with a wealth of detail events, little known incidents, ancient customs and other matters of which she was completely ignorant in her current incarnation.

Cases, also thus recorded, of children who, in full waking consciousness, remember details of their past lives — as in the classical case of Dr. Semona's twin daughters — possess an even greater evidential value. These cases for the most part deal with children who, dying in their early years, are almost immediately reborn, thus making more likely the recollection of their former lives.

A FORMER HOME DISCOVERED

The case of Madame Raynaud, for some time assistant to Dr. Durville of Paris, offers convincing evidence of the theory of reincarnation. Madame Raynaud's memories of her former life arose spontaneously, in normal waking consciousness, and these memories were afterward found to have been correct in every detail.

From her earliest childhood, Madame Raynaud was haunted by the vision of an old house of peculiar architecture, situated in a beautiful park, under the clear blue skies of a southern land. On the terraces of this house, she saw herself walking to and fro, sad and dejected, a prey to persistent ill-health, and she affirmed that she had died there of consumption a hundred years before in her twenty-fifth year.

In 1913, Madame Raynaud went to Italy for the first time, and on arriving at Genoa immediately recognized it as the place of her former incarnation. The friends of Dr. Durville, with whom she was staying, at once volunteered to help in the search for her former home; but it was Madame Raynaud who guided them in their drive through the town and finally led them to the house she had so often seen in her waking dreams.

"Here it is! this is the place where I lived and died a hundred years ago," she cried, as a sudden bend in the road revealed the entrance gates of an old country house.

"Why," said her host, "this is the mansion of the family S... They are well known in Genoa, and it should not be difficult to make inquiries about the people who lived here in the last century."

On the evening of that day Madame Raynaud, whose psychic faculties seemed to have become enhanced by the sight of her former home, suddenly exclaimed, "I was not buried in a cemetery as other people are: my body rests in a church: I feel sure of it."

Circumstances did not allow Madame Raynaud to prolong her visit to Genoa, but after her return to Paris, Dr. Durville made careful inquiries among his Italian friends, with the following result: In the archives of the Church of San Francisco d'Albaro, Genoa, are kept minutes of all the death certificates of the parish in which is situated the house of the S. . . . family. Among these certificates was found the following entry, a copy of which was sent to Dr. Durville:

23rd October 1809

"The Lady Joanna S. . . . , widow of De B. . . . for the past few years residing at her house in Albaro, always sickly, and whose ill-health was, during these last days, aggravated by a chill, died on the 21st instant, with all the Sacraments of the Church; and today, with our permission in writing, and with the authorization of the Mayor, also in writing, her body was privately transported to, and buried within, the Church of Our Lady of the Mount."

(The usual signatures are appended.)

It will be noticed that this death certificate confirms Madame Raynaud's story on three important points: the approximate date of her death, her prolonged ill-health and the unusual fact that her remains had been buried in a church instead of the Genoa cemetery.

Before these details were made known to Dr. Durville, thus excluding the possibility of unconscious telepathy, a sensitive whom he had hypnotized in the hope of obtaining details of Madame Raynaud's past life, at once described Genoa; discovered the Lady Joanna; spelt, with some hesitation, her family name; affirmed that she was now reincarnated; then suddenly exclaimed: "Why, is it possible? It is Madame Raynaud. . . . They are merged one in the other. . . . They are one and the same."

REUNION AFTER QUICK REBIRTH

Many other recorded instances exist of recollection of former lives. One remarkable case is recorded in Delhi, where a young Hindu girl of eight and a half years of age was successful in tracing the whereabouts of her old home and the relatives of her past life. The story, as personally verified by a well known member of the Theosophical Society, was printed in *Theosophy in India,* Jan.-Feb. 1936, when the case was still attracting attention.

The girl for the first three years of her childhood did not talk. She appeared gloomy and contemplative. From her fourth year she began to speak about her home at Mathura, a place about 100 miles away from Delhi, but the parents and relatives paid little heed. The child's teachers pronounced her quite intelligent and some three or four years later a neighbor, an advocate and close friend of the family, decided to investigate the case.

The girl was in the habit of saying that in her old home she had plenty of sweets, fruit and money. She even described in detail the business of her husband, the location of the house, its plan and the coloring of its walls. She referred to her relatives and when her husband was mentioned she used to bow her head in the customary respect. Although she gave the name of her brother-in-law, she would not utter that of her husband, as is also customary in India. She stated that she had been the mother of two children, the first of whom died while she was living, while she herself passed away from her last physical life ten days after the birth of the second child, a son.

Pressure was brought to bear upon her to give the name of her husband to enable the advocate friend of the family to make further investigations. Her girl friends with whom she played were asked to put the question to her, and for one of them she wrote the name on a slip of paper as K. C. of Mathura. This information had to be confirmed and during the interval she continually asked her parents to take her to Mathura, her old home. Once during a lesson she began to cry and begged her teacher to take her to Mathura. The teacher was considerate and told her that it was not possible for this to be done unless she gave the name and address of her husband. Once more she wrote her husband's name on a slip of paper as K. C. and handed it over to her teacher. This convinced the parents that her information was correct and the advocate friend wrote a letter to Mr. K. C. at Mathura making him acquainted with the facts of the case, little knowing that corroboration would be forthcoming.

After a few days Mr. K. C. replied that the incidents of his life related by the girl were correct and suggested a meeting with his brother, who was then in Delhi on business. The girl at once identified him as her husband's brother, and from questions and answers which followed it was found that the detailed description of the house and the circumstances of the death of Mr. K. C.'s wife were correct in their entirety. The girl also showed keen desire to proceed to Mathura with her brother-in-law (of the past life), but as the two families were not even friends, this could not be arranged.

MEMORY OF DETAILS CONFIRMED

Mr. K. C. was naturally interested in the case and a little later he came down to Delhi from Mathura with his son (born to the girl in her past life) to see the young lady for himself. As soon as she saw him, she burst into tears and bowed her head in respect. Questioned as to who the two persons were, she did not hesitate to say that one was her husband and the other was her son. She gave details of the husband's likes and dislikes, and accurately described the moles and other marks on her husband's body. Mr. K. C. confirmed every statement of the girl, to the great surprise of the friends and relatives collected in the house. The girl and the boy at once became great friends and seemed very happy together. Very strong evidence was thus given that the girl must have been Mr. K. C.'s former wife, even though she had reincarnated within 2¼ years of the passing away of her previous physical body.

In order to reduce any shock which a sudden parting might have given to the young girl, the advocate took the party for a drive through New Delhi. At every opportunity the girl and the boy played together and were obviously very happy in each other's company. Indeed, the advocate friend, who had seen the girl from her infancy, stated that he had never seen her so happy as on this occasion.

Further evidence, if not proof, was given that the girl was indeed a reincarnation of the former wife. Before the party left for the ride, she approached her mother and gave her instructions that certain dishes were to be prepared for the guests and that these were to be served before their final departure. On returning from the drive, Mr. K. C. was surprised, and to some extent shocked, to see that his old favorite dishes which his deceased wife used to prepare for him were placed before him. Mr. K. C. had to admit that, as the young girl had claimed, he and his wife were a loving pair and the wife was greatly devoted to him.

LEGAL ACCEPTANCE OF MEMORY OF PAST LIFE

Another account of apparently proven memory of a former life appeared in *Adventures in Arabia,* by W. B. Seabrook.[1]

"Every soul has previously passed through many human incarnations. . . . The most interesting of the incarnation cases I heard was the story of a certain Mansour Atrash. It is vouched for by dozens of persons in the Djebel. This Mansour Atrash married a girl of twelve, by the name of Ummrumman, Mother of the Pomegranate. Shortly afterward he was killed in a raid. Those events occurred about thirty years ago. At the exact hour of his death, a fact afterward verified, there was born to a family of Druses hundreds of miles away,

[1]From *Adventures in Arabia* by William Seabrook, Copyright 1927, by Harcourt Brace & Co., Inc., (U.S.A. and Canada); George G. Harrap & Co., Ltd., (British Commonwealth).

in the mountains of the Lebanon, a boy, whom they named Najib Abu Faray. He grew to be twenty years of age without ever leaving his native mountains, and then by accident was taken to the Djebel Druse, the old home of Mansour Atrash. As soon as he reached the mountain, he said: 'I must be in a dream. I have seen all these places before; they are more familiar than my own mountains.' When he came to the village in which Mansour Atrash had lived, he said: 'This is my village, and my house is up a certain street and on a certain corner.' He walked through the twisting streets, straight to the house of Mansour Atrash, went to a walled-up recess, had the bricks torn down, and discovered a small bag of money that he remembered having put there in his former life. Later he was taken to some vineyards belonging to the Atrash family, where there were disputed boundaries. He pointed out the boundaries that he said he had laid when he was Mansour Atrash, and a Druse court of law accepted them. He had now given so many proofs of his identity that he was recognized by the children of Mansour Atrash as their reincarnated father and received ten camel-loads of grain as a present from the Atrash family."

MEMORY CORROBORATED

Life Digest (May 1944), in an article entitled *This Boy Had Lived Before,*[1] published the following example of memory of a former life:

In the later half of 1922, a three-year-old Indian boy

[1] Originally published in *Answers,* London.

named Vishwa Nath, of Bareilly, India, surprised his parents by giving them minute details of what he claimed was his previous life. The boy pestered his father about a place called Pilibhit, wanting to know how far it was from Bareilly, and begging his father to take him there. His father and mother, believing (quite erroneously) that children with such memories die young, tried everything in their power to make the boy forget his strange fancies. But as he grew older his preoccupation with his past life grew more intense. Yielding to the boy's entreaties, his parents took him to the Government High School in Pilibhit. The boy said he did not recognize the school. It was, in fact, a new building.

Vishwa Nath then astounded his hearers with a wealth of information about his previous life in Pilibhit. He said his neighbor had been a Lafa Sunder Lal, who boasted of a green gate, a sword and a gun, and who held nautch parties in the courtyard of his house. He said his father had been a landowner with a great fondness for wine, rohu fish and nautch girls. He claimed that he had studied in the government school, passing in Urdu, Hindi and English, and reaching the sixth class. All this was subsequently confirmed as correct. He described the house in which he had lived, including its interior, and when he was taken to the building everything was exactly as he described it, including the position of a staircase. The little boy put his finger correctly upon a man in a group photograph as being Har Narain, finally capping his amazing memory of another life by pointing to himself — a boy seated in a chair. The boy in the photograph was Laxmi Narain, son of Babu Nai Narain, who had died of lung trouble at Shajehuenpur, on December 15, 1918, at the age of thirty-two. Among other details given correctly by Vishwa Nath were the exact site of class six in the local school, the appearance of his teacher, the names of places where he had worked and the name of his personal servant. The boy's maternal uncle corroborated many of these statements, including facts everyone else had forgotten.

MEMORY AND FACULTY RECOVERED

H. Fielding Hall, author of *The Soul of a People,* vouches for the case of a little girl of seven who told him in detail the story of her previous incarnation, in which she said she had been a man who ran a marionette show. To test her, her parents brought her a marionette doll. She at once manipulated the strings quite correctly, although she had never seen a marionette before. "I have been married four times," she said. "Two of my wives died, one I divorced, and one was living when I died, and is living still. I loved her very much indeed. The one I divorced was a very dreadful woman." Pointing to a scar on her shoulder, she added: "See this? She took up a chopper and cut me."

Fielding Hall made some inquiries and found that a birthmark on the child corresponded exactly to a mark which had been given to a former owner of a marionette show by his wife, who had been traced. The divorced wife and the much-loved wife were still living, and when asked why she did not go to live with the "wife" she loved so much, the little girl replied: "But that was all in a former life." In addition, the child accurately described places and people living great distances away that she had never seen and had known only in her previous life.

A REBORN SOLDIER

The following case was printed in *The American Magazine,* New York, of July 1915:

> This . . . story was written by a commercial photographer of Minneapolis. The photographer is the elder sister of little Annie and up to the time of the incident neither she nor any of the family believed in or knew anything of the doctrine of rebirth.

> Annie, my little half-sister, younger by 15 years, was a queer little mite from the beginning. She did not even look like any member of the family we ever heard of, for she was dark almost to swarthiness, while the rest of us all were fair, showing our Scotch-Irish ancestry unmistakably. As soon as she could talk in connected sentences she would tell herself fairy stories, and just for the fun of the thing I would take down her murmurings with my pencil in my old diary. She was my especial charge — my mother being a very busy woman. I was very proud of her. These weavings of fancy were never of the usual type that children's fairy tales take; for, in addition to the childish imagination, there were bits of knowledge in them that a baby could not possibly have absorbed in any sort of way.

> Another remarkable thing about her was that everything she did she seemed to do through habit and, in fact, such was her insistence, although she was never able to explain what she meant by it. If you could have seen the roystering air with which she would lift her mug of milk when she was only three and gulp it down at one quaffing you would have shaken with laughter.

This particularly embarrassed my mother and she reproved Annie repeatedly. The baby was a good little soul and would seem to try to obey and then in an absent-minded moment would bring on another occasion for mortification. "I can't help it, mother," she would say over and over again, tears in her baby voice, "I've always done it that way."

So many were the small incidents of her habits of speech and thought and her tricks of manner and memory, that finally we ceased to think anything about them and she herself was quite unconscious that she was in any way different from other children. One day when she was four years old she became very indignant with father about some matter; and as she sat curled up on the floor in front of us, announced her intention of going away forever.

"Back to heaven where you came from?" inquired father with mock seriousness. She shook her head.

"I didn't come from heaven to you," she asserted with that calm conviction to which we were quite accustomed now. "I went to the moon first, but — you know about the moon, don't you? It used to have people on it but it got so hard that we had to go." This promised to be a fairy tale, so I got my pencil and diary.

"So," my father led on, "you came from the moon to us, did you?"

"Oh, no," she told him in a casual fashion. "I have been here lots of times — sometimes I was a man and sometimes I was a woman!"

She was so serene in her announcement that my

father laughed heartily, which enraged the child, for she particularly disliked being ridiculed in any way.

"I was! I was!" she maintained indignantly "Once I went to Canada when I was a man. I 'member my name, even."

"Oh, pooh-pooh," he scoffed, "little United States girls can't be men in Canada! What was your name that you 'member so well?"

She considered a minute. "It was Lishus Faber," she ventured, then repeated it with greater assurance, "that was it — Lishus Faber." She ran the sounds together so that was all that I could make of them — and the name stands in my diary today — Lishus Faber.

"And what did you do for a living, Lishus Faber, in those early days?" My father then treated her with the mock solemnity befitting her assurance and quieting her nervous little body.

"I was a soldier" — she granted the information triumphantly — "and I took the gates!"

That is all that was recorded there. Over and over again I remember we tried to get her to explain what she meant by the odd phrase but she only repeated her words and grew indignant with us for not understanding. Her imagination stopped at explanation. We were living in a cultured community, but although I repeated the story to inquire about the phrase — as one does tell stories of beloved children, you know — no one could do more than conjecture its meaning.

Someone encouraged my really going further with the matter and for a year I studied all the histories of

Canada I could lay my hands on for a battle in which somebody took the gates. All to no purpose. Finally I was directed by a librarian to a "documentary" history, I suppose it is — a funny old volume with the s's like f's, you know. This was over a year afterwards, when I had quite lost hope of running my phrase to earth. It was a quaint old book, interestingly picturseque in many of its tales, but I found one bit that put all the others out of my mind. It was a brief account of the taking of a little walled city by a small company of soldiers, a distinguished feat of some sort, yet of no general importance. A young lieutenant with his small band — the phrase leaped to my eyes — "took the gates". And the name of the young lieutenant was "Aloysius LeFebre".

Thus, although such detailed memories are the exception rather than the rule, they demonstrate that past lives are not necessarily forgotten.

INSTINCT AS MEMORY

Admittedly, physical memory of incidents of past lives is rare, but of memory as far as innate capacity and knowledge are concerned there is complete evidence in both the animal and the human kingdoms of nature. A theosophical explanation of animal instinct is that it is a form of memory. The soul, or consciousness, evolving through ducklings, for example, has evolved through other ducks in earlier times and knows instinctively that ducks can swim. In the new brain, the ducklings do not remember those previous existences, but they have brought over the instinct which results from them and so, quite naturally, they swim. Similarly, all instinctive habits and customs in the animal kingdom are attributable to race memory.

Domestic animals frequently display old habits which belonged to their earlier phases of evolution, when they were still in a wild state. The dog, for example, will frequently turn round and round before he lies down because, in earlier days as wolf, he had need to tread down his jungle or forest bed to make it comfortable. Like the duckling he does not remember but follows his instinct, even though in his case the need for the action has vanished.

In much the same instinctive fashion, we human beings "remember" our past lives. Our inherent "gifts" — actually hard won faculties — our natural sympathies and our antipathies, are remembrances of the past. Love at first sight — that love which springs suddenly into existence and may last for a life-time — is but the spontaneous renewal of an ancient tie. There are others for whom we feel an inborn antipathy which also has its roots in other lives, when the relationship was not a happy one. We thus bring with us into each new incarnation intuitive rather than detailed memory of old associations. The fruits of these experiences manifest themselves in the new personality as innate faculties, sympathies and antipathies which would otherwise be difficult to explain.

CHAPTER VII

CHILD GENIUS

THIS brings us to the third problem; that of child prodigies. The phenomenon is well typified in the following accounts:

BOY OF EIGHT CONDUCTS 80-PIECE ORCHESTRA

"The eight-year-old Italian conductor Ferruccio Burgo made a triumphant debut with a symphony orchestra at the Carnegie Hall on Saturday. The curly-headed boy in knee pants showed no signs of nervousness as he conducted an 80-piece orchestra in five operatic overtures and Beethoven's First Symphony.

"Professional critics praised his good sense of rhythm, notable musical memory and feeling for melody. He first conducted publicly at Fiume at the age of four."

(Extract from *The New Zealand Herald*, March 2nd, 1948.)

SCOTTISH CHILD PRODIGY

"Carol Gallacher, a seven-year-old Glasgow school-girl, who could sing the *Marseillaise* in French when she was two years old and whose current reading is Plato's *Republic* and Sir Thomas More's *Utopia*, is arousing the interest of leading child psychologists in all parts of Britain.

"One of them recently set Carol an intelligence test in which university honors graduates had averaged 145 marks. Carol scored 181 marks.

"The director of the Child Psychology Clinic, who supervised the test, said: 'This child is undoubtedly a genius. She should have a wonderful future.'

"Although she read Thackeray's *Vanity Fair* and Swift's *Gulliver's Travels* when she was only four years old, Carol still likes to play with dolls. The cinema sends her to sleep.

"Many child prodigies have shown great aptitudes in music. These include Mozart, who composed minuets before he was four; Beethoven, who played in public at eight, and composed works which were published at ten; Hummel, who gave concerts at nine; Schubert, who composed at eleven; Chopin, who played a concerto in public before he was nine; Mendelssohn, Brahms and Dvorak, who showed exceptional talents early; Richard Strauss, who wrote a polka and a song at six; and Samuel Wesley, who played the organ at three and composed an oratorio at eight."

(Extract from *The New Zealand Herald*, January 28th, 1948.)

Mozart, Music's Wonder Child
By Donald Culross Peattie

" 'Positively the last concert. . . . The boy, not yet seven, will perform on the harpsichord, play a concerto for violin, and accompany symphonies on the clavier, the keyboard being covered with a cloth, as easily as if he could see the keys. He will name all notes sounded at a distance, singly or in chords, and improvise on harpsichord and organ as long as desired. Tickets ½ taler.'

"Thus did a notice in a German newspaper in 1763 advertise, as if he were a side-show freak, the most universal genius of music the world has ever known, Wolfgang Amadeus Mozart. In the audience sat another boy, the 14 year-old Goethe, destined too to become immortal. Years later he could still recall the far-off bright picture of the merry-faced little musician who ran to the bench before the harpsichord in his absurd, exquisite costume of lilac satin, with powdered wig and tiny sword, and flung his heart into the glittering notes.

"Born with absolute pitch, infallible rhythm, and natural comprehension of harmony, Master Mozart had come into this world with an inexplicably complete gift. That is how, at the age of four, the child began to learn to play the clavier (a forerunner of the modern piano) and at five picked up a violin, and reading at sight, staggered through six trios with his father and a friend.

"This child read and wrote notes before he could do as much with letters. Compositions dating from his sixth year are recognizable from the opening bars as the music of Mozart and nobody else. Graceful and sure, spirited, precise and brave, they are the work of a unique stylist and a great soul. . . ."

(Extract from *The Readers' Digest,*
February, 1947.)

The doctrine of reincarnation solves the problem that child prodigies present. Their strange genius has been brought over from former lives, in which mastery of their subjects had been attained. In a new life, having thereby earned the right to, and so obtained, a parentage and a body through which their acquired genius can be expressed, they display their unusual faculties early in life.

CONSCIOUS RECOVERY OF MEMORY

The full memory of all former lives is preserved, not in the brain of each successive body but in the consciousness of the Ego, the individual, immortal *continuum,* the inner Self. To bring this memory within reach of the brain, a mental feat must be performed. The power must be acquired to dissociate oneself consciously from the physical, emotional and the mental bodies and to identify oneself with the Ego. Normally, we are accustomed to identify ourselves with our bodies, while in reality these are only vestures worn by the true man. The brain is but an instrument, thought the power which drives it, the Spiritual Self of the thinker being the source of the intelligence from which that thought arises. He who would gain first-hand knowledge of philosophical and spiritual truths must dissociate himself from the body and in deep meditation realize his Spiritual Selfhood, know himself as the Inner Ruler Immortal within the body. Since every detail of the past is known to the Ego, full memory of that past can thereafter be attained.

The primary purpose of meditation is to exalt physical brain consciousness into union with the Self within. This can be done and the process is a scientific one. Raja Yoga,[1] the science of union, must first be studied and its principles applied. The resultant experience leads man to his own

[1] *An Introduction to Yoga,* A. Besant.

personal realization of the essential truths of religion and philosophy. He is then endowed with a faith that is no longer blind but founded upon first-hand knowledge, and therefore unshakable. The full memory of past lives having been regained, reincarnation ceases to be a theory. Thereafter it is known as a fact in nature.

THE PERFECTIBILITY OF MAN

One other objection sometimes raised when questioning the verity of the doctrine of rebirth, concerns the necessity for a return to earth after death. It is argued that the stature of the perfect man can be attained in the spiritual worlds without the need for rebirth. In answer, it is pointed out that the terms "perfection" or "adeptship" imply not only spiritual and intellectual, but physical perfection as well. The Adept has mastered and perfected his physical body and is able to maintain it in full health for a period far beyond the normal allotted span. He is also master of all the forces and energies of nature and possesses complete knowledge of natural laws and processes. This attainment is only possible as a result of direct experience. Just as one cannot learn to swim or fly by theory alone, but must practice in the appropriate element, so physical mastery and perfection can only be obtained as a result of physical experience.

THE SOLUTION OF THE PROBLEMS

The doctrine of reincarnation and karma are thus seen to provide logical solutions of the four problems to which attention is drawn in Chapter I.

There is not, cannot be, undeserved human suffering. Every experience is the product of preceding action by the individual to whom the experience comes, whether that action was performed in a former, or in the present life.

The goal of human existence is the attainment of the stature of the perfect man, and this attainment is assured to the Spiritual Self of every human being.

Child prodigies are not chaotic sproutings from the tree of human life. They are demonstrations of the fact that every individual man has lived before, has striven and attained in preceding incarnations. In rare instances the fruits of that attainment force their way through the childish brain and body, and, when parents and teachers are sensible enough to recognize the significance of the phenomenon, a reasonable measure of intelligent training enables the past genius to flower early in the new life.

People who say that they remember past lives are in no sense enigmas to reincarnation. When their descriptions are supported by fact and testimony, they are correctly recalling incidents of former lives.

CHAPTER VIII

THE ESSENTIAL DOCTRINE

THE four problems having been solved and some prevalent
objections met, we can now proceed to an examination of the
doctrine itself. Reincarnation is based upon a combination of
a doctrine concerning human life and a principle in nature.
The doctrine — already expounded — is the perfectibility of
man and the principle is periodicity. Man, in his essential
spiritual nature, is as a seed of Deity. That seed is "planted"
in the superphysical and physical worlds in order that it may
develop to the highest possible degree. In the human kingdom
of nature, the individual who has reached this state is known
as an Adept, or perfect man.

TIME AND OPPORTUNITY

Clearly such achievement is not possible in one earthlife. Even if the full span be completed, there is neither time
nor opportunity in which fully to develop every human
power. This difficulty is met by the operation of the principles of periodicity, ebb and flow, forthgoing and return.
Solar systems, including even their minutest components,
obey this law. Similarly, not once but many times, man as
Ego enters into physical incarnation at birth and withdraws
therefrom at death. On each occasion variations of sex, race,
caste, environment, opportunity and activity occur. As a

result, progress is made in each life, until at last all necessary experience is gained, all powers developed and all weaknesses overcome. By this means ultimate success for all men is assured, infinite time and wide diversity of experience being thus provided for the unfolding Spiritual Self of every man. Each cycle on the ascending spiral path by which man reaches his goal of adeptship, consists of a descent of a portion of the power, life and the consciousness of the Ego into physical incarnation and a subsequent return, always to a higher position on the spiral.

THE DESCENT INTO INCARNATION

Each new cycle opens as a result of a change of consciousness experienced by the Ego, at a certain period after the conclusion of the preceding cycle. This change is called in Eastern philosophy *tanha,* a Sanskrit word meaning thirst for life; in this case the thirst is for further growth, wider and fuller self-expression. Knowing that these can only be gained by re-entry into physical life, the Ego, which abides on the plane and level of consciousness of the abstract intellect, turns his attention to the denser worlds. A triple ray of egoic power, life and consciousness is projected first to the plane of the concrete mind, where mental substance is drawn round it, gradually forming a mental body. Meanwhile the ray penetrates still further into the realm of emotion where, similarly a body of desire is formed. Finally it reaches the physical world and, generally at the time of conception, is attached to the first twin cell then formed, which later grows into a physical body.[1] During pre-natal life these bodies de-

[1] *A Study in Consciousness*, A. Besant, *The Miracle of Birth*, Geoffrey Hodson.

velop and the Ego becomes increasingly conscious of them. After birth this process continues, egoic awareness at the three levels steadily improving, particularly from the seventh year. Normally, egoic mastery of the physical body reaches its height at full maturity.

THE LIFE AFTER DEATH

This process of growth through physical experience continues until death, the moment and manner of which are governed by the law of cause and effect. The physical body is then laid aside and the process of return begun. For a time, the length of which depends in large measure upon the nature and strength of the emotional life while on earth, the Ego is conscious in the emotional body and continues to reap karma at that level. This, no doubt, gives rise to the idea of purgatorial experiences after death. Valuable lessons are learned, evolutionary progress is made, and eventually the desire body is laid aside and the last stage of the return journey entered upon. This consists of life in the mental body which, being completely free from desire, is perfectly happy, a state corresponding to some extent to paradise or heaven in religious teachings.

Eventually, when the higher aspirations have found their fullest possible mental expression, this period comes to an end and the aspect or fragment of the Ego which has made the cyclic journey is re-absorbed into the higher Self from whence it came. The human prodigal son has returned home.[1]

The Ego then becomes temporarily quiescent as far as the

[1] *Through the Gateway of Death*, Geoffrey Hodson.

three lower worlds are concerned. During this period, all experiences and achievements of the cycle just concluded are
converted into faculty, gift and capacity, into power, wisdom
and knowledge. These harvestings of the life cycle are preserved as imperishable possessions of the Ego, and constitute
part of those "treasures in heaven, where neither moth nor
rust doth corrupt, and where thieves do not break through
nor steal"[1] — the true riches of the soul.

THE ATTAINMENT OF NIRVANA

Such, in part, is a single cycle in the spiral ascent of man
to the fulfillment of his destiny. Perfection attained, he is free
from "the wheel of birth and death," all necessity for further
human, physical experience having been outgrown. This liber-
ation is beautifully expressed in *The Light of Asia,* Sir Edwin
Arnold's poem on the life of the Lord Gautama Buddha, the
great Eastern teacher and sage. Therein, the state of perfection is described as follows:

> "No need hath such to lives as ye name life;
>   That which began in him when he began
>   Is finished: he hath wrought the purpose through
>   Of what did make him Man.

> "Never shall yearnings torture him, nor sins
>   Stain him, nor ache of earthly joys and woes
>   Invade his safe eternal peace; nor deaths
>   And lives recur. He goes

[1]Matt. VI, 20.

"Unto NIRVANA. He is one with Life,
  Yet lives not. He is blest, ceasing to be.

OM, MANI PADME, OM! the Dewdrop slips
  Into the shining sea!"

The teaching that the necessity for further rebirth is eventually outgrown, would appear to be echoed in the words of the Book of Revelation: "Him that overcometh will I make a pillar in the temple of my God, and he shall go no more out." (Rev. III, 12.)

CHAPTER IX

THE LAW OF CAUSE AND EFFECT

THE doctrine of natural causation or karma is intimately associated with that of the spiritual evolution of man to perfection through successive lives on earth. Under karmic law every human action, mental, emotional or physical, produces an exactly appropriate reaction. These reactions are, however, not always received in the same life in which the acts were committed. In such cases they remain in abeyance until, in a later incarnation, conditions arise in which they can be justly and appropriately experienced; for the exactness of the operation of the law of cause and effect demands that causes must produce their effects at the level, on the plane and in the world in which the cause was generated. Physical actions produce physical effects. Emotional, mental and spiritual actions produce their effects in their appropriate worlds. Since every physical action of one life cannot produce its full reaction during that lifetime, a return to earth is necessitated in order that the essential condition, namely awareness in a physical body, can be established. St. Paul would seem to refer to this rule in his words following his enunciation of the law of sowing and reaping: "For he that soweth to his flesh (unto his own flesh — R. V.), shall of the flesh reap corruption, but he that soweth to (unto — R. V.) the Spirit shall of the Spirit reap life everlasting." (Gal. VI, 8.) According to this view, the merits and demerits of previous lives determine the conditions of the present one. Each man generates the causes of which his later experiences are the effects.

SPECIAL CREATION, CHANGE OR LAW

Three theories have been advanced to explain the diversities, the inequalities and the apparent injustices of human birth and opportunity. One of these is the theory of special creation, by which each new-born baby is regarded as a newly-created being. This view, held in certain schools of Christian thought, is in many ways unsatisfactory, especially since the only solution offered to the problem of the apparent injustices of life is that they are the will of God and that life and death are mysteries into which it is not lawful to probe. Also, it must be admitted, souls without a past springing suddenly into existence out of nothing, yet with marked mental and moral peculiarities, often distinct from those of the parents and other members of the family, are a conception as unacceptable as would be the corresponding idea of babies suddenly appearing from nowhere, unrelated to anybody and yet showing marked individual, family and racial characteristics.

CHANCE

The second theory advanced is that of chance. Sir Walter Scott tells of a laughing philosopher who compared human life to a table pierced with holes, each of which has a peg made exactly to fit it; but, since these pegs are stuck in haphazard and without regard to their corresponding holes, the most awkward mistakes inevitably result from this chance arrangement. Some people believe that a similar chance determines our bodily and environmental conditions at birth and afterwards.

To the thoughtful this theory, like the first, is profoundly unsatisfactory. Why should human life be the one thing in the manifested universe which is not governed by law?

Throughout all nature, from the densest matter to the most subtle ether, from our own planet to the furthest star, from infusoria to solar systems, science discovers exact law. Speaking in London in 1929, Sir Arthur Eddington, then Professor of Astronomy at the University of Cambridge, said of the law behind the forces of the material universe: "It is perfect and unbreakable, and worthy to be associated with the mind of God."[1] In view of the existence of exact law throughout the physical universe, it is hardly reasonable to assume its absence in the selection of the conditions of human birth and the life which follows. Such absence would also contradict the teachings of wise men throughout the ages, and particularly the Hermetic principle: "As above so below."

LAW

The third of the three explanations of the diversities of human experience remains — that of law. According to this, conditions of human life, whether of health, happiness, capacity and opportunity, or of disease, sorrow, weakness and limitation, are the results of the operation of exact law, are reapings from past sowings. Combined, the doctrines of reincarnation and karma provide a solution of the problem of the inequalities of human birth and opportunity consistent with logic and justice. The divergences and differences in bodily and mental condition and capacity, and the varied environments into which men are born and in which they live, are the direct results of their own preceding conduct.

H. P. Blavatsky states: "There is the *Karma* of merit and

[1] *Science and the Unseen World*, a lecture at the Friends' Meeting House, Euston Road, London, England.

the *Karma* of demerit. *Karma* neither punishes nor rewards, it is simply *the one* Universal LAW which guides unerringly and, so to say, blindly, all other laws productive of certain effects along the grooves of their respective causation . . . causes which are undying, *i.e.,* which cannot be eliminated from the Universe until replaced by their legitimate effects, and wiped out by them, so to speak, and such causes, unless compensated during the life of the person who produced them with adequate effects, will follow the reincarnated Ego, and reach it in its subsequent reincarnation until a harmony between effects and causes is fully re-established."[1]

HARMONY AND DISCORD

Karma, though abstract and intangible, is the foundation on which the concrete and sensory universe is built. It produces those modifications of the One Mind of which individuality consists and from which the experience of egohood arises—an illusion, since, from the point of view of the highest reality, no division into units is conceivable. Adversity is the result of a disturbance in the stillness of the universal Intelligence, a discord in nature's harmony. Disturbance is caused primarily by selfish human thought, inevitably discordant within the major mind, which is selfless, impersonal, harmonized, still. From every movement there must follow a return to the stillness which preceded it and out of which it arose. From every discord there must be a return to harmony. Karma — the effect of action — consists largely of this enforced return.

The function of the law is to maintain the perfect rhythm

[1] *The Theosophical Glossary; Karma.* H. P. Blavatsky.

by which the One Mind is made manifest. When that rhythm is broken, the law instantly exerts a reattuning influence and it is this function which produces pain. Discordant actions are those performed under the illusion that each man is a separate being. The way of freedom from pain consists in the conquest of the illusion. He whose every thought is a harmonized expression of the Divine Mind and through whom that mind functions perfectly, meeting no barrier of separative individuality — such a man is ever in bliss.

Nevertheless, during a certain evolutionary phase, the experience of individuality is not in itself an evil; rather is it a stage of growth, corresponding in the plant to the formation of the stem from which branch, leaf and flower later give full expression to plant life. Individuality becomes a source of pain only when it is over-accentuated or unduly prolonged, to produce selfishness, undue competitiveness, conflict. When man fights aggressively at any level, he disturbs the harmony of the One Mind. The law then comes into operation, restoring that harmony by a force which is irresistible. Man's attempted resistance to this process, even though unconscious, increases the severity of his suffering. Immediate self-correction and surrender to the law are the most effective mental measures for the reduction and ultimate removal of pain. Hence the value of knowledge of this doctrine.

THE WAY OF PEACE

Buddhism teaches that the obstacles to the attainment of "good"[1] karma may be removed by observance of the follow-

---

[1]Presumably meaning happiness-producing, since all karma must be good because educative. The law "moves to righteousness." (Light of Asia.)

ing five precepts, which are expressed in the moral code of Buddhism: (1) Kill not; (2) Steal not; (3) Indulge in no forbidden sensual pleasure; (4) Lie not; (5) Take no intoxicating or stupefying drug or liquor.

The cause productive of misery is stated in that religion to be desire, the craving—constantly renewed—to satisfy oneself without ever being able to secure that end. The destruction of that desire, or the estranging of oneself from it, and the steadfast adoption of the Noble Eightfold Path, bring about self-emancipation from pain, sorrow, misery.

This Path consists of: Right Belief; Right Thought; Right Speech; Right Action; Right Means of Livelihood; Right Exertion; Right Remembrance; Right Meditation, which leads to spiritual enlightenment or the development of the Buddha-like faculty which is latent in every man. This was summed up by the Lord Buddha himself as: to cease from all sin; to get virtue; to purify the heart.[1]

This sequence of right conduct and assured happiness is not regarded as a reward from some extra-cosmic deity or other divine benefactor, but solely as the result of the impersonal operation of the law of cause and effect or karma.

The two doctrines of reincarnation and karma are thus found to provide a completely satisfying philosophy of life. They answer otherwise insolvable problems and perplexities. Rightly understood and intelligently applied, they also provide a strong incentive to self-discipline and an infallible guide to the attainment of health, happiness, and self-liberation from the wheel of birth and death with all its miseries and to discovery of the sure path leading to the fulfillment of life.

[1] *The Buddhist Catechism*, Henry S. Olcott. 44th edition, pp. 93-94.

CHAPTER X

KARMA IN THE BIBLE

THE doctrine of karma is also an essential component of Judaism and original Christianity, however much it may be repudiated by exponents of the latter to make room for the doctrine of vicarious atonement which it would nullify.[1] This is demonstrated by the following quotations from the Scriptures of both those religions:

> "Even as I have seen, they that plow iniquity, and sow wickedness, reap the same."   (Job IV, 8)

> "For they have sown the wind, and they shall reap the whirlwind."   (Hosea VIII, 7)

> "Ye have plowed wickedness, ye have reaped iniquity."   (Hosea X, 13)

> "Even so every good tree bringeth forth good fruit; but a corrupt tree bringeth forth evil fruit."
> (Matt. VII, 17)

---

[1]Not, however, in the sense of at-one-ment, the Lord Christ having unified himself with the Spiritual Soul of every human being. Thus at one with all, he shares with each his perfected light and life. By this means, he enhances the power of the spiritual over the material man, thus reducing or "saving from" tendencies to sinfulness. Despite the varying degrees of responsiveness to this *perpetual* ministration, he, the Lord of love and compassion, continues without intermission on his sacrificial at-one-ment on behalf of every human being.

"The Lord is known by the judgment which he exe-cuteth: the wicked is snared in the work of his own hands."   (Psalms IX, 16)

"Also unto thee, O Lord, belongeth mercy: for thou renderest to every man according to his work."
(Psalms LXII, 12)
(Also Proverbs XXIV, 12)

"I the Lord search the heart, I try the reins, even to give every man according to his ways, and according to the fruit of his doings."   (Jeremiah XVII, 10)

"Therefore I will judge you, O house of Israel, every one according to his ways, saith the Lord God . . . "
(Ezekiel XVIII, 30)

"Great in counsel, and mighty in work: for thine eyes are open upon all the ways of the sons of men: to give every one according to his ways, and according to the fruit of his doings."   (Jeremiah XXXII, 19)

"For the Son of man shall come in the glory of his Father with his angels; and then he shall reward every man according to his works."   (Matt. XVI, 27)

"Who will render to every man according to his deeds."   (Romans II, 6)

"Tribulation and anguish, upon every soul of man that doeth evil . . ."   (Romans II, 9)

"But glory, honour, and peace to every man that worketh good . . .

For there is no respect of persons with God.

For as many as have sinned without law shall also perish without law; and as many as have sinned in the law shall be judged by the law;

For not the hearers of the law are just before God, but the doers of the law shall be justified."

(Romans II, 10-13)

"For we must all appear before the judgment seat of Christ; that every one may receive the things done in his body, according to that he hath done, whether it be good or bad."   (2 Cor. V, 10)

"And if ye call on the Father, who without respect of persons judgeth according to every man's work . . ."

(1 Peter I, 17)

". . . I will give unto every one of you according to your works."   (Rev. II, 23)

"And I saw the dead, small and great, stand before God; and the books were opened; and another book was opened, which is the book of life; and the dead were judged out of those things which were written in the books, according to their works."

(Rev. XX, 12)

"And, behold, I come quickly, and my reward is with me, to give every man according as his work shall be."

(Rev. XXII, 12)

"So then every one of us shall give account of himself to God." (Romans XIV, 12)

"The fathers shall not be put to death for the children, neither shall the children be put to death for the fathers; every man shall be put to death for his own sin." (Deut. XXIV, 16)

". . . The son shall not bear the iniquity of the father, neither shall the father bear the iniquity of the son; the righteousness of the righteous shall be upon him, and the wickedness of the wicked shall be upon him." (Ezekiel XVIII, 20)

God said:
"Whoso sheddeth man's blood, by man shall his blood be shed." (Genesis IX, 6)

Christ said:
"For verily I say unto you, till heaven and earth pass, one jot or one tittle shall in no wise pass from the law, till all be fulfilled." (Matt. V, 18)

"And it is easier for heaven and earth to pass, than one tittle of the law to fail." (Luke XVI, 17)

"Judge not, that ye be not judged. For with what judgment ye judge, ye shall be judged: and with what measure ye mete, it shall be measured to you again." (Matt. VII, 1 and 2)

"Therefore all things whatsoever ye would that men should do to you, do ye even so to them; for this is the law and the prophets."   (Matt. VII, 12)

"God is not mocked; for whatsoever a man soweth that shall he also reap."   (Gal. VI, 7)

CHAPTER XI

REINCARNATION IN WORLD THOUGHT

> Nay, but as when one layeth
> His worn-out robes away,
> And, taking new ones, sayeth,
> "These will I wear to-day!"
> So, putteth by the spirit
> Lightly its garb of flesh,
> And passeth to inherit
> A residence afresh.
>
> *The Song Celestial,* SIR EDWIN ARNOLD

I, Buddh, who wept with all my brothers' tears,
  Whose heart was broken by a whole world's woe,
Laugh and am glad, for there is Liberty!
  Ho! ye who suffer! know
Ye suffer from yourselves . . .

The Books say well, my Brothers! each man's life
  The outcome of his former living is;
The bygone wrongs bring forth sorrows and woes
  The bygone right breeds bliss.

That which ye sow ye reap. See yonder fields!
  The sesamum was sesamum, the corn
Was corn. The Silence and the Darkness knew!
  So is a man's fate born.

He cometh, reaper of the things he sowed,
    Sesamum, corn, so much cast in past birth;
And so much weed and poison-stuff, which mar
    Him and the aching earth.

If he shall labor rightly, rooting these,
    And planting wholesome seedlings where they grew,
Fruitful and fair and clean the ground shall be,
    And rich the harvest due ...

Such is the Law which moves to righteousness,
    Which none at last can turn aside or stay;
The heart of it is Love, the end of it
    Is Peace and Consummation sweet. Obey."

The Light of Asia, SIR EDWIN ARNOLD

God generates beings, and sends them back over and over again, till they return to Him.

The Koran (Holy book of Islam)

And when his body falleth off altogether, as an old fish-shell, his soul doeth well by the releasing, and formeth a new one instead ... Ye who now lament to go out of this body wept also when ye were born into it ... The person of man is only a mask which the soul putteth on for a season; it weareth its proper time and then is cast off, and another is worn in its stead ... I tell you, of a truth, that the spirits which now have affinity shall be kindred together, although they meet in new persons and names.   *The New Koran*

After leaving this body a virtuous man acquires a still better place and body and his wisdom constantly increaseth.

Jam-i-Kaikhoshra (Zoroastrian text)

(Pythagoras) was accustomed to speak of himself in this manner; that he had formerly been Aethalides . . . At a subsequent period, he was reborn as Euphorbus, and was wounded by Menelaus at the siege of Troy, and so died. In that life he used to say that he had formerly been Aethalides; and that he had received as a gift from Mercury (God of Wisdom) the memory of his soul's transmigrations . . . also the gift of recollecting what his own souls and the souls of others had experienced between death and rebirth.

Life of Pythagoras (582-507 B.C.), DIOGENES LAERTIUS

What Pythagoras wished to indicate by all these particulars was that he knew the former lives he had lived, which enabled him to begin providential attention to others and remind them of their former existences.

Life of Pythagoras, IAMBLICHUS

Lives follow without resembling one another, but a pitiless logic links them together. Though each of them has its own law and special destiny, the succession is controlled by a general law, which might be called the repercussion of lives . . . There is not a word or action which has not its echo in eternity, says a proverb. According to esoteric doctrine, this proverb is literally applied from one life to another.

Pythagoras and the Delphic Mysteries, EDOUARD SCHURE

All these souls, after they have passed away a thousand years, are summoned by the divine ones in great array, to the Lethean river . . . In this way they become forgetful of the former earthlife, and re-visit the vaulted realms of the world, willing to return again into living bodies.

The Aeneid, VIRGIL (70-19 B.C.)

If there be nothing new, but that which is
Hath been before, how are our brains beguiled,
Which laboring for invention, bears amiss
The second burthen (bearing) of a former child!
O, that record could with a backward look,
Even of five hundred courses of the sun,
Show me your image in some antique book,
Since mind at first in character was done!
That I might see what the old world would say
To this composed wonder of your frame;
Whether we are mended, or whether better they,
Or whether revolution be the same.
    O, sure I am, the wits of former days
    To subjects worse have given admiring praise.

Sonnet, WILLIAM SHAKESPEARE

I have been here before,
    But when or how I cannot tell;
I know the grass beyond the door,
    The sweet keen smell,
The sighing sound, the lights around the shore.
You have been mine before, —
    How long ago I may not know;
But just when at that swallow's soar

Your neck turned so,
Some veil did fall, — I knew it all of yore.

Sudden Light, DANTE GABRIEL ROSSETTI

The Body of B. Franklin,
Printer
Like the Cover of an Old Book,
Its Contents Torn Out
And
Stripped of its Lettering and Gilding,
Lies Here
Food for Worms,
But the Work shall not be Lost,
For it Will as He Believed
Appear Once More
In a New and more Elegant Edition
Revised and Corrected
By the Author.

BENJAMIN FRANKLIN
(Epitaph written at the age of twenty-two).

We wake and find ourselves on a stair; there are other stairs below us, which we seem to have ascended; there are stairs above us, many a one, which go upward and out of sight. But the Genius which according to the old belief stands at the door by which we enter, and gives us the lethe to drink, that we may tell no tales, mixed the cup too strongly, and we cannot shake off the lethargy now at noon day. Sleep lingers all our lifetime about our eyes.

Experience, RALPH WALDO EMERSON

I know I am deathless,
I know this orbit of mine cannot be swept by a carpenter's
    compass . . .

And whether I come to my own to-day or in ten thousand or
    ten million years,
I can cheerfully take it now, or with equal cheerfulness I can
    wait . . .

To be in any form, what is that?
(Round and round we go, all of us, and ever come back
    thither) . . .

Births have brought us richness and variety,
And other births will bring us richness and variety . . .

And as to you, Life, I reckon you are the leavings of many
    deaths,
(No doubt I have died myself ten thousand times before.)

Song of Myself, WALT WHITMAN

Towards the end of a long life, filled with reading, thinking
searching for its explanation, I have yet to find a solution
that solves its problems better than the explanation of reincarnation. No saner solution, covering all the facts, presents
itself. A few years ago, talking in the shadow of the pyramids
with one of the clearest minds in England, in Europe for
that matter, his words come back to me in this connection
. . . My friend said suddenly: "We have no proof, nor ever
shall have. Survival must always remain a subject for specula-
tion . . . Of all the systems the world has yet devised, I know

one only that offers a satisfactory explanation of the complex problems of existence — reincarnation. It is logical, just, complete. It holds water . . ."

"On Reincarnation", ALGERNON BLACKWOOD

The doctrine of Reincarnation is one of the great historical solutions to the problems which Life sets to the human imagination. It is an answer to the deep desire of the spiritually awakened soul for divine justice . . . for an order of existence in which the suffering and apparent injustice of this world shall be abolished, and . . . for an opportunity of self-redemption and self-purification, not so much from what is generally called "sin," as from the spiritual lethargy which appears to be a condition of continued physical existence itself . . .

The doctrine of Reincarnation, as I understand it, is an attempt to declare the final triumph of the spiritual life. If we imagine . . . that no human soul is perdurably doomed, we must needs have a religious system which offers the opportunity of redemption to all, and *continues to offer it until the redemption of all is accomplished.* Those who are now blind to the necessity of the spiritual life must journey on till their eyes are at last opened. And there is no denying that the doctrine of Reincarnation declares this in a form acceptable to the ordinary imagination.

"Reasonableness and Practicality of Reincarnation,"
JOHN MIDDLETON MURRY

A flower blossoms; then withers and dies. It leaves a fragrance behind, which, long after its delicate petals are but a little dust, still lingers in the air . . . Let a note be struck on an instrument, and the faintest sound produces an eternal echo. A disturbance is created on the invisible waves of the shoreless ocean of space, and the vibration is never wholly lost. Its energy being once carried from the world of matter into the immaterial world will live for ever. And man, we are asked to believe, man, the living, thinking, reasoning entity, the indwelling deity of our nature's crowning masterpiece, will evacuate his casket and be no more! Would the principle of continuity which exists even for the so-called *inorganic* matter, for a floating atom, be denied to the spirit, whose attributes are consciousness, memory, mind, LOVE! Really, the very idea is preposterous . . .

The doctrine of *Metempsychosis* has been abundantly ridiculed by men of science and rejected by theologians, yet if it had been properly understood in its application to the indestructibility of matter and the immortality of spirit, it would have been perceived that it is a sublime conception. If the Pythagorean metempsychosis should be thoroughly explained and compared with the modern theory of evolution, it would be found to supply every "missing link" in the chain of the latter. There was not a philosopher of any notoriety who did not hold to this doctrine, as taught by the Brahmans, Buddhists, and later by the Pythagoreans.

Isis Unveiled, H. P. BLAVATSKY

With reincarnation man is a dignified, immortal being, evolving towards a glorious end; without it, he is a tossing straw on the stream of chance circumstances, irresponsible for his character, for his actions, for his destiny . . . The Ancient

Wisdom teaches, indeed, that the soul progresses through many worlds, but it also teaches that he is born in each of these worlds over and over again, until he has completed the evolution possible in that world . . . Truly, further evolution lies before us in other worlds, but . . . they are not open to us until we have learned and mastered the lessons our own world has to teach.

The Ancient Wisdom, ANNIE BESANT

Were an Asiatic to ask me for a definition of Europe, I should be forced to answer him: It is that part of the world which is haunted by the incredible delusion that man was created out of nothing, and that his present birth is his first entrance into life.

Parerga and Paralipomena, SCHOPENHAUER

Our duty is present with us every instant.

My doctrine is: Live so that thou mayest desire to live again — that is thy duty; for, in any case, thou wilt live again!

And in every one of these cycles of human life there will be one hour where for the first time one man, and then many, will perceive the mighty thought of the eternal recurrence of all things — and for mankind this is always the hour of noon.

FRIEDRICH NIETZSCHE

The human soul, once launched on the streams of evolution as a human individuality, passes through alternate periods of physical and relatively spiritual existence. It passes from the one plane or stratum, or condition of nature to the other under the guidance of its Karmic affinities . . . it returns to spiritual existence . . . for rest and refreshment and for the gradual absorption into its essence, as so much cosmic progress, of the life's experience gained "on earth."

A. P. SINNET

The man is an Ego, an imperishable circle in the sphere of Divinity . . . He has lived on earth in many a past life, and there thought and felt and acted both good and evil; he has set in motion forces that help or hinder both himself and others . . . Time may pass us by, and we grow old and "die"; but that is only an illusion. We are immortal souls, and the world's history is only the alphabet of our speech, and we fashion the future as we *will* to fashion it . . . For this is the power the Divine Wisdom gives to all who love her — to greet life in all time not as the elders of the sunset, but as the children of the dawn.

Theosophy and Modern Thought, C. JINARAJADASA

The Lord let the house of a brute to the soul of a man,
And the man said, "Am I your debtor?"
And the Lord, — "Not yet; but make it as clean as you can,
And then I will let you a better."

By An Evolutionist, ALFRED, LORD TENNYSON

CHAPTER XII

PREDESTINATION AND FREE WILL

The subject of predestination and free will has deeply occupied the minds of scholars and students. Part of the theosophical contribution to the solution of the apparent paradox would seem to be that there are at least two universal forces at work upon man under which he is virtually powerless. One of these is evolutionary pressure at all levels of his existence from within outward such as that, for example, which physically applied, produces an oak from an acorn. The other force perpetually resolves into harmony all discordant conditions, continually corrects imbalance.

The principle of unfoldment under the irresistible pressure of a propellant energy operates from within the innermost essence of the universe, and the spiritual seeds or germs (Monads) of all beings. The process of the maintenance of harmony is ceaselessly active throughout the universe and all it contains. This harmonization operates upon man as a sequence of cause and effect, under which discordances created by his selfish and cruel actions, for example, are forcibly resolved and harmony is restored.

These two powers — unfoldment from less to more and reharmonization — operate irresistibly upon man, as upon all else that exists. Man can delay or hasten, but he cannot ultimately frustrate these two functions of the cosmic Will.

The operation of the universal law of cyclic expansion and evolution is irresistible. In these two natural processes man is helpless, in them he is predestined. In due course man as Monad must reach the stature of perfected and harmonized manhood. Similarly every human action, modified by subsequent actions, will inevitably bring about an exactly appropriate reaction upon the actor. In this man is indeed powerless, and so predestined.

This predestination need not in the least disturb the minds of those who become aware of it, for the simple reason that the two inner impulses — to expand and to harmonize — arise from within the Spirit-Self of man, which is identical with the Spirit-Self of the universe. Once the concept is removed of an external, controlling Deity separate from man, the sense of compulsion then vanishes; for if man is predestined, then he is self-predestined, which removes all stigma from the fact. If man's future is predetermined, then he himself is the only predeterminator and is, moreover, predestined by the action of his own free will.

Perfect happiness is utterly certain for man if he voluntarily collaborates with these two cosmic procedures — perpetual unfoldment and the maintenance of harmony. He who orders his life to the end of the most harmonious and speedy evolutionary progress at all levels will generate no friction, and so find peace. The man who always acts harmoniously, never unnecessarily injuring any other being, and who within himself is ever harmonious and a harmonizer, is assured of freedom from the painful reattuning process. He does not provoke the retaliation of the law. Ever deepening harmony and happiness will be his. A Greek proverb says: "He who is obedient to the law, the gods lead gently by the hand. Those who resist, they drive mercilessly."

Thus, though fundamentally self-predestined, restriction and suffering are by no means inevitably pre-ordained for man. He creates them for himself and he can, therefore, do away with them for himself. In these ways man can be free and the great Teachers who have visited mankind have, by both example and precept, shown him the way of freedom.

The problem of predestination and free will may perhaps thus be regarded, and the apparent paradox which they seem to present be partially resolved. Other factors are, however, also involved.

EPILOGUE

THE twin doctrines of causality in human affairs and man's evolution to perfection through successive earthly lives are important to some minds for two reasons. First, they provide a logical solution of otherwise insoluble human problems and second, they make possible a belief, based on reason, in both assured justice and a noble destiny awaiting every man — perfection of the power to help.

The two doctrines are indeed indispensable to the mental peace of the humanitarian who is also a logician; for without reincarnation and the compensatory law, the ephemeral nature of human life and the inequalities of human experience pose a riddle which defies rational solution. Together, they throw upon man's existence a flood of light in which it can be fully comprehended from its inception, through its evolution, its tribulations and its happinesses and on to its glorious goal.

Thus mentally illumined, man, with courage born of reason, can face the difficulties and trials of life; for he knows his own preceding hurtful actions to be their sole causes and harmlessness to all creatures, including his own body, to be their sure prevention.

Perspective and true evaluation enable the reincarnationist to enjoy fully the lights of the picture of life and at the same time to recognize the equal significance of the shadows; for he knows both lights and shadows to be educative in the true meaning of the word. The sufferings of mankind are seen to be comparable to the storm on Galilee, without which the sleeping Christ might not have been awakened; for by their very stress, the storms of human life awaken into action man's dormant powers. Employing these, he develops the capacity both to still the storms within himself and to render effective aid to his storm-tossed fellow men.

Reincarnation and karma thus provide an inspiring and logical philosophy of life which may be simply stated in four postulates:

> Perfected manhood is the assured destiny of the Spiritual Self of every man.

> Reincarnation, as the evolutionary method, provides the necessary time and opportunity for self-perfecting.

> The law of action and constantly modified reaction insures justice to all men.

> The attainment of perfection is rendered certain by the interior presence of an infinite, divine power ceaselessly at work within the Spiritual Self of every human being.

These principles form a basic part of the metaphysical system known as Theosophy which has been well defined, I think, as "an esoteric synthesis of known religions and philosophies."

Theosophy is not, I suggest, ever to be regarded as a completed system to be accepted as such. On the contrary, as must be true of everything organic and spiritual, Theosophy cannot have a fixed geometrical outline, the whole of which can, as it were, be traced on paper by rule and compass. Certain aspects, such as the existence of the eternal Self and experiences of oneness, refuse to be objectively defined; for this would be setting a limit to both truth itself and to man's capacity to discover it as interior experience.

The Lord Buddha evidently wished to guard against any such limitation, for he said: "Do not believe in a thing said merely because it is said; nor in traditions because they have been handed down from antiquity; nor in rumors, as such, nor in writings by sages, merely because sages wrote them . . . nor on the mere authority of your own teachers and masters. But we are to believe when the writing, doctrine, or saying is corroborated by our own reason and consciousness."

Examined, Theosophy is found to include a complete philosophy of life which, accepted and applied, gives meaning and purpose to human existence, shows the causes in human actions for human successes and failure and, therefore, the way in which failures may be diminished, eventually to occur no more. Theosophy "teaches" also, for example, that man is essentially a spiritual being, his mind and his body being only temporary means of self-expression and self-unfoldment. When this true Self is discovered and becomes the directing power, there is permanent peace for both the individual and the race. Without that discovery, it is affirmed, peace is impossible for either of them. The search for and discovery of the Self is therefore presented as of supreme importance.

The meaning and the purpose of human life is stated to be the evolution of the Spiritual Self of man to successive "perfections" through successive lives on earth, and this is advanced as the true purpose of his existence. The great variety of experiences arise because they are all decided by preceding actions under the operation of the law of cause and effect. Simply put, cruelty brings war to nations and pain and disease to individuals. There is no possible escape from this sequence. Inversely, kindness brings happiness and health; and until this law is recognized and accepted as a rule of life, there will, it is said, continue to be both war and disease. If this is true, then the existence and operation of this law must, as quickly and fully as possible, be understood by humanity at large; for there will be no enduring peace, happiness, and health until it is totally recognized and implemented.

The above references to peace draw attention to the theosophical contribution to this pressing and perplexing problem. The unity of all life is affirmed, the Spirit within all men being one Spirit. Each man belongs to one spiritual race which is without divisions of any kind. This being true, "each man exists for the sake of other men." (Einstein) These ideas are regarded as of very great importance, for experience of this unity, and its application to human life, are said to constitute the only possible means whereby lasting peace can be established on earth, and assured health and happiness be attained by every human being.

Other books by Geoffrey Hodson

Angels and the New Race
Hodson believes that angels will play an important role in the future of mankind.

The Call to the Heights
A teacher to pupil book of instructions on how to awaken our higher consciousness.

The Christ Life from Nativity to Ascension
New—New Testament—intuitional insights.

The Hidden Wisdom in the Holy Bible, Volumes I, II, III.
Volume I: The life of Jesus. Volume II: The Book of Genesis. Volume III: The Book of Genesis continued.

The Kingdom of the Gods
A clairvoyant views the angelic kingdom. With 29 full page illustrations in b/w and full color.

Man's Supersensory and Spiritual Powers
The structure and nature of our transcendental powers.

Meditations on the Occult Life
The path of discipleship; the life of the aspirant.

Music Forms
The occult value of music. Complete with b/w and full color illustrations.

Occult Powers in Nature and Man
Hodson relates the universal creative processes to the spiritual nature of man's true Self.

These titles are available from:
QUEST BOOKS
306 West Geneva Road
Wheaton, Illinois 60187